Cover
Espalier by Mary White, 1953

Illustrations
Taken from and inspired by Hints for Housewives,
Peter Jones leaflet, c.1950's

All proceeds from this book
will go to the John Lewis Foundation

Contents

Great British ingenuity

The British have always been famous for having a spirit of 'make do and mend'. During the Blitz, wartime housewives became experts at making the most out of powdered egg and stretching their scarce resources with creative tricks. Fastforward 65 years, and we now understand that resources aren't infinite, and it is once more a matter of pride to be economical and practical with what we have. That's not to say that indulgence is off the list; it just means that everyday wasteful ways are no longer palatable.

At John Lewis we have always ensured that our customers are given the best support when it comes to expert insight and advice. Our shop floor staff are more than happy to spend their time answering queries or helping customers make a considered purchase. Our haberdashery departments and in-store sewing and knitting classes further illustrate our commitment to keeping traditional and essential skills alive and relevant.

We realised however, that somewhere along the line, the information that our grandmothers had at their fingertips had been mislaid: how to keep your clothes in their best condition; how to save a beloved jacket with missing buttons and how to treat your home and planet more kindly – good intentions are in abundance, but knowledge is sadly lacking.

With this in mind, we've asked all of our 28,000 Partners – not only those who work on the shop floor, but also those in our call centres, offices, and even some who've retired (or thought they had!) – to share their top tips. We've collected the best in this handy book, taking inspiration from that popular wartime adage, 'make do and mend'. As well as rediscovering tried-and-tested classics, we've found brilliant new approaches that make perfect sense in our modern, gadget-filled world. As well as helping to make what you already own last longer, and ensuring you make the best purchase first time, we hope to reignite the simple pleasure of domestic achievement that taking care of, rescuing or reinventing your favourite items can bring.

Home truths

Try these canny, tried and true techniques
around the home

- "Keep pesky ants away with a chalk line – they won't cross it". Simply draw a boundary around outside entry areas and "watch it work wonders but don't forget to re-draw it after rain".

- Deter flies the gentle way with mint – the ultimate summertime herb for the kitchen windowsill.

- Never throw away a fresh herb plant again. Herbs freeze very well; just place in a plastic bag in the freezer and crumble into dishes as you need them.

- Freeze fresh chilli peppers in a plastic food bag to stop them going wrinkly. Use as needed – no need to thaw. "But keep your hands away from your eyes, and wash them thoroughly afterwards".

- Use ice cube trays to freeze any leftover wine – "if you've got any!" This means you can add a glass to casseroles and stews without the need to open a full bottle.

- Create an "ice and a slice in one" to add to summer drinks: simply slice up lemons and limes, arrange in layers on a baking tray, and freeze.

- Stop your salt cellar from clogging up by adding a few grains of rice to absorb any moisture.

- For truly flavoursome tomatoes, treat them as the fruit that they are and place them in a fruit bowl. They taste much better at room temperature than straight from the fridge.

- Electric and ceramic hob rings stay hot for a long time; "turn them off a minute or two early, put a lid on your pan and the food will go on cooking".

- Stale bread is as useful as fresh. Slices can be turned into easy summer or bread and butter puddings, while medium-sized chunks make great croutons for soups and salads, and crumbs are perfect for breading chicken or fish. Sliced loaves can also be frozen until you need a slice which can go "straight from the freezer to the toaster".

- Hot fat poured down the plughole can solidify and block pipes. Instead; "mix it with cheap oatmeal, let it set until hard, and encourage birds to enjoy the treat by scattering the mixture in the garden".

- For a cost-effective cleaner, use bicarbonate of soda on a damp cloth to get worktops and surfaces spotless. Treat tough stains by making a paste with a little water and leaving it on the stain for a couple of hours before wiping away.

- Getting rid of strong flavours is easy; rub chopping boards with a cut lemon to banish lingering onion or fish smells.

- A drop of baby oil on a soft cloth will take smears off stainless steel, chrome or aluminium. Rub gently, then wipe clean with a second soft cloth.

- To get rid of the smell of garlic on your hands, rub them along a stainless steel sink or a warmed stainless-steel teaspoon. "Sounds silly but it really works".

- To shift stubborn deposits at the bottom of a wine decanter, add crushed eggshells and a little water, swill round briskly, turn out and rinse well. "Works a treat!"
- White vinegar lifts limescale from stainless steel sinks and plugs. Leave it to act briefly before scrubbing, then rinse well.
- To clean an oilcloth or vinyl table covering, sponge clean as normal, dry off and then spray with furniture polish. "A quick buff and the cloth will look as good as new".

- A quick scour with salt and an old toothbrush is a simple way to freshen up stained mugs or cups.
- Before cleaning your oven, place an ovenproof dish containing a solution of equal parts of water and vinegar inside at the back, then turn the temperature on low for ten minutes. As the solution evaporates, the vinegar loosens grime, which will wipe off easily once the oven has cooled.
- To remove lingering smells from your microwave, place half a lemon in

a bowl of water and heat on low power for a couple of minutes. Then clean as normal.

• Use aluminium kitchen foil for cleaning solid silver cutlery. Line a plastic bowl with foil, shiny side up. Add a mug of washing soda crystals and top up with hot water. Making sure you wear rubber gloves, gently drop in the cutlery. It will turn shiny bright within a couple of minutes. Rinse cutlery under running warm water, then dry with a soft cloth. "Only use this method if you are certain the entire item is solid silver, as it can lift silver plate".

• Always rinse cutlery immediately after use as prolonged contact with salt, vinegar, egg, tomato juice and acidic fruits can cause pitting and staining.

• "To make scented candles last longer, light them for only 20 minutes before guests arrive and then extinguish". The heat from the wax will allow the fragrance to be released long after the flame has gone out.

• When measuring for your new curtains, add 6 inches (15cm) above and 6−8 inches (15−20cm) either side to the size of your window. This will allow for your track or pole and for decent curtain coverage on both sides.

• Maintaining your mattress can keep you free of back pain and allergies. Prevent a sagging mattress by turning it once a month and keep dust mites at bay with regular cleaning and airing, and by fitting a mattress protector. Most standard mattresses should be changed every seven years.

- Television screen size and the size of your room should be considered together to create an optimum viewing experience. For best results, use the following guide:

Best viewing distance from TV	TV screen size
Under 8 ft (2.5m)	17–26in (43–66cm)
8–10ft (2.5–3m)	28–32in (72–82cm)
10–13ft (3–4m)	36–42in (92–107cm)
Over 13ft (4m)	42–50in (107–127cm)

- To remove dust from plasma screens and computer monitors, wipe very gently with a soft cloth, as any pressure can leave marks. Avoid spray polishes. If in any doubt, use a specialised screen wipe. "A used sheet of fabric softener will also do the trick and will prevent dust from resettling".

- Avoid mounting a plasma screen television above a working fireplace. Direct exposure to heat can damage the screen, as the gases contained beneath it are flammable.

- When choosing garden furniture, tropical hardwoods such as teak, iroko and courbaril have a high oil content, so they can stay outside all year round. A natural fading of the wood's original colour is normal, and an annual wash with soapy water to remove pollution and algae is all that is needed. "If you choose to apply oil, make sure that the timber is completely dry, or the wood may blacken".

- During the winter months, outdoor cushions and parasols need to be stored away from the elements. To keep them at their best, wash with an upholstery shampoo once a year and store in a dry place – but avoid polythene bags as they may cause mould.

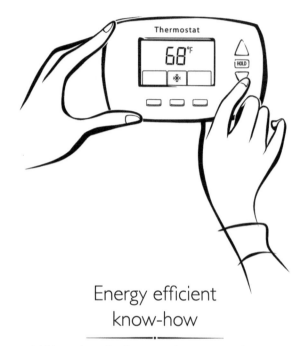

Energy efficient
know-how

Without knowing it, most of us consume energy
that we don't need. A few thoughtful actions can reduce
everyday energy usage and spend

• Set your water thermostat
at a temperature you like
to bathe or wash dishes in.
"This way, your boiler won't
have to waste energy
heating itself when you
will only add cold water
to the hot later".

- Clean water is precious, so think about ways in which you could cut down on your consumption. Don't leave the tap running while you clean your teeth and wash your vegetables in a bowl, not under running water.
- Save water by using your cup to fill the kettle so you only boil exactly what you need for a cup of tea.

- Make sure the cooling elements on the back of your fridge are dust free. Dust prevents them from releasing heat easily, which means that they have to use more energy to get the job done.
- Adding dryer balls to your tumble dryer will soften fabrics and cut down on lint and wrinkles. "Also, using dryer balls saves a whopping 25 per cent in energy consumption".
- Metallic reflectors behind radiators are "a low tech but highly energy efficient way of pushing heat back into the room rather than into the walls". Aluminium foil is a cheap alternative – attach a sheet to the wall, making sure the shiny side is facing the radiator but not touching it.
- Insulate windows and conserve precious heat with heavy curtains. You can add special insulating linings with detachable curtain tape.
- Invest in rechargeable batteries and a charger.

They quickly recoup their costs – "especially with battery-hungry kids' toys".

- Save energy by getting into the habit of doing a regular 'charger check'. When not charging an appliance, unplug the charger from the wall socket or it will keep drawing electricity regardless of whether the appliance is attached or not.

- Invest in an intelligent energy-saving adapter plug. Plug your PC into one of its three sockets and all your peripherals (printer, modem, scanner, etc) into the others. This clever device will only supply power to your accessories once it detects that the computer is switched on. Not suitable for use with laptops.

- An electricity monitor makes it simple to identify the most power-hungry appliances in your home, and where you could cut back.

- USB memory sticks are portable, easy to use and can be re-used indefinitely; "much less waste than blank CDs and DVDs".

- To get the maximum life out of your digital camera, mobile phone or laptop, let the battery run down fully before recharging. Constantly charging a partly-charged appliance will reduce the life of its battery.

Fashion fixes

Whatever your personal style, clean, smart,
well-maintained clothes are essential for creating a good
impression. Try these tricks for looking your best

- Elastic bands wound
around the ends of a coat
hanger will prevent delicate
garments from slipping
to the floor and becoming
crushed.

- Ward off moths by placing
a few drops of grapefruit
or lavender oil on a pad
of kitchen paper or a
handkerchief and leaving
it at the back of your

wardrobe. "Take care to position it where it won't stain garments".

- When storing woollies, remember that moth grubs survive washing. Kill them off by freezing clothes in a plastic bag for a day or so before storing.

- To maximise the life of your suits, alternate on a daily basis and always hang on wooden hangers. "You will then only need to dry clean once every six months".

- To prevent a mohair jumper shedding hairs, before wearing, place it in a plastic bag, and put it in the freezer for a couple of days".

- To prevent terminal fraying on a favourite shirt, snip the edge clean, then apply Fray Check, a clear liquid that hardens and keeps threads in place.

- Don't try to rub away lily pollen that has brushed onto clothing as it will leave a stain. Instead, dab very gently with sticky tape to lift the powder away, then position in direct sunlight for a few hours. More often than not, the pollen will completely disappear.

- To remove chewing gum stuck to a piece of clothing, put the garment in the freezer for a few hours; the gum will harden, and can then just be snapped off.

- Sprinkle a little bicarbonate of soda into your trainers; "it's a great chemical-free deodorant".

- Reinvigorate badly scuffed leather shoes by rubbing with half a raw potato. Then wipe clean and polish as usual.

- Shine up your shoes with the inside of a banana skin. Allow to dry, then buff with a soft cloth.

- A button adjuster lets clothes out about an inch. "Perfect during early pregnancy or after a large Sunday lunch!"
- Use saddle soap to remove watermarks from leather shoes. "Resist the temptation to dry them by a fire or radiator as this can harden or distort the leather".

- Rolled-up magazines make great boot 'trees'. They'll keep your boots upright and in good shape.
- 'Toupee tape' is a great fashion fix for gaping clothing. It can attach fabric to skin, or to another fabric, such as a bra; "just make sure you don't leave it on the fabric for longer than

24 hours". You can find this in a haberdashery department.

- Ladders in tights can be stopped in their tracks with a dab of clear nail varnish.

- Give faded jeans a new lease of life with a blue dye made for use in the washing machine (also available in black). To remove residual dye from your washing machine, run a hot cycle with a cup of soda crystals.

- Well fitting shoes help to protect children's feet; the 28 hard bones that make up adult feet are still only soft cartilage until children are 18, and as the nerves are buried deep in a child's foot, they cannot always tell if shoes are pinching them and causing irreparable damage. Even tight-fitting socks can cause problems, so make sure the sock is the appropriate size for the child's age.

Laundry day

This essential laundry know-how will keep
your clothes in mint condition

• Most wear-and-tear that
happens to clothes is easily
avoidable. Often, we only
consider the temperature
of a washing cycle, and
not the type of fabric we
are washing, which is just
as essential. Many washing
detergents now provide
excellent results at a
temperature of only 30°C;
however, it is still important
to match the right cycle to
the right fabric; the wrong
agitation in the machine can
cause bobbling and fading.

Washing

Cotton cycle
Maximum
temperature 30°C
Normal wash

Synthetic cycle
Maximum
temperature 30°C
Mild wash

Wool cycle
Maximum
temperature 30°C
Very mild wash

- Look after your hard-working appliances. A filter clogged with fluff means your washing machine or dryer has to use more energy to get the job done. Maximise efficiency by emptying the filter once a month.

- A musty-smelling washing machine can be freshened up with a cup of soda crystals. Pop them into the detergent dispenser and run it empty on a hot wash cycle.

- Always mend clothes before putting them in the wash; the agitation of the machine cycle can make a tear or pull worse.

- Elastic and lace trimmings in lingerie can be damaged in the washing machine. Protect delicate items by putting them in a net bag before loading. "A pillowcase will do the job too; just tie at the top, or fit with a drawstring".

- Pillow protectors placed under your pillowcases extend the life of your pillows, and are easy to throw in with the rest of the wash as necessary.

- Keep net curtains looking fresh and bright white by soaking them overnight in cold water and detergent before washing.

- Loosen a curry stain by applying a glycerin solution, available from chemists. Dilute 1 part glycerin to 2 parts water, leave for about an hour to soften the stain, then wash as normal.

- Tackle an ink stain by squirting it with hairspray, then work a solution of water and white vinegar into it until it comes out, before washing as normal. Not suitable for silks or delicate fabrics, "but perfect for school shirts".

- To make it easier to iron sheets that have dried and creased, try folding them up, putting them in a plastic bag, and popping them in the freezer overnight. "Cotton and linen iron best when damp".

- Delicate dresses and shirts can be hung on the back of the bathroom door. "The gentle steam from the shower will help the creases drop right out".

Rescue, repair and reinvent

Everything can become a little worn around the edges;
a few small but bright ideas can come to the rescue

Remember

- Test new cleaning methods on an inconspicuous spot
- Protect your hands from harsh substances with rubber gloves
- The quicker you treat a stain, the easier it is to remove

- A rub with toothpaste can get rid of fine scratches on a watch face or on delicate glassware. Once applied, buff vigorously. Toothpaste will also clean jewellery beautifully. Using a soft toothbrush, rub gently onto silver, gold or gemstones. Then wash carefully, and polish with a dry cloth "until they sparkle like new again".
- Metal polish can help reduce scratches on acrylic surfaces. Apply and then rub with a soft cloth.
- Use car wax to shine up the fronts of tired-looking white goods, such as fridges and washing machines. "It's great for making scratches look less prominent".
- Reclaim unworn jewellery. Simple jewellery repairs are easy to do yourself. Use replacement earring hooks, backs, clasps, and little chains to lengthen tight necklaces. "You'll find these in a haberdashery department".
- Never throw away an old toothbrush; they're great for cleaning around taps or tackling tricky corners.
- Clean stainless steel bathroom fixtures by pouring a liberal amount of rubbing alcohol directly on them (you can get it from a chemist). "This not only makes them sparkle but also kills all the germs".
- "A plastic bag melted onto the side of a hot toaster or hob can be cleaned off with nail-polish remover". Make sure the appliance is

switched off and has cooled down. Not suitable for use on plastic appliances.

- To make a bobbly jumper look as good as new, invest in a cordless fabric shaver or wool comb. If the garment seems beyond repair, turn it inside out and cut off the arms. "Sew up the arm holes, neck and waist and reinvent it as a quirky cushion cover".

- To help your curtain track run more smoothly and to make it last longer, clean with a regular household detergent, then spray with a silicone-based lubricant.

- Don't lose precious memories such as photographs if something happens to your computer. Invest in an external hard drive to back up your files. This will also free up more memory on your computer and help it run faster.

- A baby-bottle sterilising tablet makes a good toilet cleaner for stubborn stains. Drop a tablet into the bowl and leave it to work for a pristine finish. "It will bring it up like new".

- "Every home needs a can of WD40, the all-purpose lubricant". Spray onto a stubborn label or sticky residue, leave for a few minutes, and watch the label swiftly slide off. Apply to crayon marks and grimy patches on walls and hard surfaces, then clean off with a little washing up liquid. "You'll need minimal elbow grease – it's amazing". Not suitable on wallpaper or fabric.

- Documents that have been through home office shredders can be used to pack delicate objects in boxes or to "make five-star bedding for hamsters and guinea pigs".

- To tackle a spill on the carpet, first scrape up any residue with a blunt knife or spoon, then blot up liquids with a clean white cloth or kitchen paper. Sponge with a teaspoon of washing powder dissolved in half a pint of lukewarm water. Blot dry but do not rub, then brush up the pile. Cover with a clean cloth to dry, and finally vacuum the area.

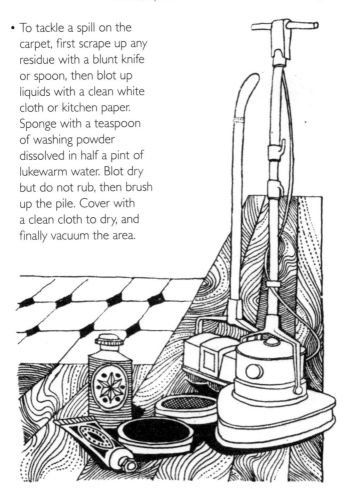

- To get candle wax off fabrics and carpets, first remove as much as you can, then cover with brown paper and a tea towel. Press with a hot iron, moving the paper and tea towel around. "Miraculously, the paper absorbs the wax".

- To get rid of persistent smells on carpets and upholstery, dab them with a paste of bicarbonate of soda and warm water. "This works brilliantly for spilt milk and pet smells".

- Don't grab the nearest coloured paper napkin to blot spills on carpets or fabrics. The colour can quickly transfer and create a bigger mess than the original one.

- Reconsider worn out fabric items; just one old towel can be cut up into several super-absorbent floor cloths, and soft old T-shirts make great dusters and polishing cloths.

- Flowers will last longer if they are put in a solution of half lemonade and half water. For 'forced' roses, plunge the trimmed stems into very hot water for twenty seconds to open the blooms and prolong life.

- Parcel tape is useful for keeping food packets and boxes tightly closed and the contents fresh; strips can be reopened and sealed many times without losing their grip.

- Use crushed eggshells in the garden to ward off snails from tender plants; "they don't like crawling over the sharp edges".

- Rainwater is free and can be collected in just about anything, from a purpose-designed water butt to old empty cans. Use it during dry spells in the garden or for washing the car.

- Protect the screens of your mp3 player, mobile phone or digital camera from keys or other sharp objects with a peel-off plastic overlay, which can be cut to fit any size screen.

- Recycle plastic supermarket fruit punnets as seedling trays.
- Use clear nail varnish on the inside of metal button holes to stop them from snapping the thread.

Pins and needles

Doing your own repairs, or giving an old favourite
a new lease of life is both fun and fashionable

- Iron-on adhesive patches or motifs can cover up holes or bleach marks. Cut out fabric letters or numbers or choose from a selection of ready-made iron-on designs.
- Fusible bonding yarn is useful if you're "not nimble with a needle". Roughly sew the required area, then iron over the thread to fuse fabrics together. Available in a haberdashery department.
- Polyester thread is stronger than cotton and won't snap – perfect for sewing on

buttons. Choose a slightly darker colour than your fabric – a lighter one will show up more.

- Getting the right tools for the job is the key to its success. The higher the needle number, the smaller the needle. Sharp needles are for fine sewing. Embroidery or crewel needles have long eyes to take thicker threads. To get rid of loose threads on a garment, use a special snag-repair needle.

- Tapestry wool from a haberdashery department is great for mending knitted or woollen garments. It's hard-wearing and available in a huge variety of colours.

- Shorten lined, ready-made pencil-pleat curtains from the top; don't try to cut them from the bottom as you will have to re-mitre the corners and turn the lining up separately. Take off the tape, cut off any excess fabric, and stitch the tape back on again.

- A multicoloured thread 'plait' is handy if you don't do much sewing and don't want to buy reels of different coloured cotton. Just pull out a single strand when you need it. Available in a haberdashery department.

- Instantly fix a drooping hem with an invisible sticky strip available from a haberdashery department. "A life-saver when you don't have a needle and thread".

- Needle-threading is easier over a sheet of white paper. If you're still having trouble, "try hairspray on the end of the cotton to stiffen it".

- Don't use your sewing scissors for cutting paper as it will blunt them.

Always have an everyday pair for casual use.

- Stick-on reflective tape is perfect for making children's clothes stand out more in dull winter months, or to transform a regular jacket into something more visible for a keen cyclist.
- Invest in a personal label maker, which can produce paper, plastic or iron-on labels. Not only an essential for labelling school uniforms but also great for marking up plugs to identify easily which appliance you are unplugging. "No more worrying that you'll mistakenly unplug your fridge-freezer".
- Start an old-fashioned button jar, making sure to snip buttons from old clothes. "Replacing all the buttons on an old coat will make it feel like a brand new purchase".

A few basic stitches are all you need
to keep your favourite items ship-shape

Running stitch

Hemming stitch

Back stitch

Blanket stitch

- Work running stitch is used for basic seams and patchwork. It's made of small regular stitches. Back stitch is much stronger – see diagram.
- Hemming stitch should be invisible from the right side. Make a double fold on the wrong side of the fabric, then make small slanting stitches, picking up only a thread or two. Or use iron-on mending

tape, which also works for repairing tears – see diagram.
- Blanket stitch will neaten frayed edges. Buttonhole stitch is worked in the same way, but the stitches are closer together – see diagram.
- To sew on a button, first mark its position with a pin through the buttonhole. Using button thread, then make a back stitch on the

wrong side of the fabric and bring up where marked, to the right side of the fabric. Stitch the thread firmly through the holes of the button, then wind it round the underneath of the button several times before taking it through to the back of the fabric, and finishing it off with a couple of back stitches.

- Use two sets of thread for a button with four holes. If one thread breaks, the other will hold the button firm. Make cross or parallel stitches, but keep to the same stitch pattern all over a garment. Polyester thread is ideal for buttons as it is stronger than cotton and won't snap. You can also use elastic thread for buttons that take a lot of strain.

- To darn a sock use matching darning or tapestry wool, a long large-eyed darning needle, and a darning "mushroom". Using small running stitches, work backwards and forwards over the hole, extending the darn around its edges by about 1 inch (25mm). Aim for neat parallel threads. Then repeat, but work the other way, weaving over threads already laid down. For a stretchy darn, weave the second set of stitches on the diagonal – see diagram.

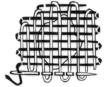

Darning stitch

In-store Classes

Check with your local John Lewis branch for classes
such as knitting and sewing.

And finally
Help others to save money by sharing your household
tips online. Set up a free Twitter account at www.twitter.com.
Subscribe to our Twitter feed @MakeDoMend2009
for regular updates.

With thanks to all John Lewis Partners who have
contributed to the making of this book.

Disclaimer
Though every care has been taken to ascertain the effectiveness of methods
and instructions given in this book, the authors and publishers cannot
guarantee the efficacy of any advice given, nor shall they be liable in the
unlikely event of any loss or damage resulting from following any advice given.

We recommend that if you are unsure about the suitability of any
of the methods listed, test them on an inconspicuous area before use.